よもすがら

All Night Long

よもすがら

All Night Long

Haiku, Senryu
  and Other Short Poems

And a Haibun on the
Great Tohoku Earthquake

by Kirby Record

Japanese Translations by
Norifumi Ida, Hidenori Hiruta and Kyoji Ishii

Banta and Pool, Publishers
BLOOMINGTON, INDIANA

Published by Banta and Pool, Publishers, Bloomington, Indiana.

Library of Congress Control Number 2013955468
ISBN: 978-0-9667237-3-1

all night long
a single drop of rain
from leaf to leaf

よもすがら
雨のしずくが
葉から葉へ

this harvest moon!
walking round and round the pond
the whole night through

名月や
池をめぐりて
よもすがら

— Matsuo Basho

Table of Contents
目次

Preface

My fascination for haiku began one evening in the International House at Indiana University, when as a student barely 17 years old, I attended a lecture on haiku by Japanese literature scholar and poet, Professor Kenneth Yasuda, who was to be my mentor and dissertation director many years later. This book is the result of more than forty years of studying and writing haiku and their related literary cousins: *senryu, renga,* and *haibun,* and other short poems, that depart from classical norms but retain the brevity of the one-breath duration and the short-longer-short pattern realized in Japanese 5-7-5 syllabic structure. The one-breath duration of the haiku corresponds to breath as a basic unit of life itself, and to the traditions that focus on an awareness of breath as the means to a heightened awareness by paradoxically transcending the senses through the senses.

Overt philosophical or linguistic intervention in the haiku mode is seen as a weakening of insight arising from direct, non-intellectualized perception of the world in its natural state. Most of the poems here are English equivalents of the haiku aesthetic: they are 5-7-5 in form, include a season word or *kigo,* and strive for an "objective" presentation of concrete imagery. Metaphor, direct statements of emotion, and overt philosophical commentary are avoided with the poems that were *intended* to be haiku. The 5-7-5 pattern in Japanese does not always translate into a clear 5-7-5 English syllable count because the English syllable is much more complex and varied in respect to duration (time of utterance) than the Japanese *onsetsu.* Many of the works in this collection do scan as 5-7-5, although some try to achieve a similar blend of symmetry and asymmetry by adopting a stress count of 2-3-2, which in my view, often approximate more accurately the effects of Japanese 5-7-5 *onsetsu.*

Traditional *senryu* also tend toward 5-7-5 but may lack the season word and are often humorous or satirical. More controversial, perhaps, are the poems that depart clearly from the direct presentation of the image—in the Pound sense, and may also lack a season word. I hope that these works will be read for their own merit and not assumed to lie within the strict haiku framework, though their debt to haiku is clear. Both the concept and term "haiku," as we now understand them, did not exist in the Japanese tradition until the late 19th century, when Masaoka Shiki first used the word to refer to an independent 5-7-5 poetic form. Previously the 5-7-5 forms were called *hokku* or *haikai,* and were integrated into the longer literary structures of *renga (haikai no renga)* or *haibun,* a prose narrative. This book includes both a *renga* or a variation of *renga* and a *haibun.* The "Monsoon Renga" is set in Malaysia and written for two voices.

The final section of the book consists of a *haibun,* based on the writer's visit to the earthquake and tsunami-ravaged area of eastern Tohoku that struck in March of 2011. In this case, the *tsunami* context is considered a substitute for an explicit season word. There is no space here for detailed discussion of the aesthetic principles and various controversies that surround haiku in English. Suffice it to say that even in Japanese, haiku has been far from one-dimensional, and that the great haiku masters themselves sometimes deviated from the norm. Basho wrote haiku that were 5-5-7 and 5-9-7, for example. What I hope for is that the works speak for themselves, and that their forms have an organic relationship to their content.

まえがき

　　　　私が俳句に魅了されたのは、インディアナ大学のインターナショナル・ハウスで、当時17歳になったばかりの学生であった私が、文学者であり詩人でもある日本人、ケネス・ヤスダ教授による俳句の講義を受けたことにさかのぼる。教授は何年もの後に私の師となり、私の博士論文の指導者になっていただいた。本書は俳句と、それに関連するいわば文学上の従兄弟とも呼ぶべき川柳や連歌、俳文、その他の詩についての40年以上にわたる研究と作品をまとめたものである。俳句の一呼吸の長さは、生命の基本単位である呼吸と呼応し、また感覚を通して感覚を超越するという逆説的な方法によって高められた意識を用いる呼吸の意識に焦点を当てた伝統とも呼応している。

　　　　俳句形式に哲学的にあるいは言語学的にあからさまに介入することは、あるがままの自然に対して、そのまま知的な詮索をしないで認識することから生ずる洞察力を弱めてしまうとみなされる。本書に掲載している大部分の詩は、俳句の持つ美学思想の英語版であって、5-7-5の形式をとり、季節を表す言葉である季語を含み、具体的な心象を「客観的に」表現しようと努めている。俳句を意識した詩では、隠喩や感情の直接的な表現、明確な哲学的分析を控えている。日本語の5-7-5の形式は、必ずしも明確な5-7-5の英語音節に対応するとは限らない。というのは、そもそも英語の音節は、日本語の「音節」に比べてはるかに長さ（表現時間）の点で複雑であり変化に富んでいるからである。本書の作品の多くは5-7-5の形式をとっているが、2-3-2の強勢リズムをとることにより、対称・非対称の融合を試みている作品もいくつかある。私の意見では、このようにすることで俳句そのものが持つ効果をより表現できると考えている。

　伝統的な川柳も5-7-5に近いが季語がなかったり、滑稽さや諷刺の要素が含まれることもある。より議論の的とのなるのはおそらく ──「古池」の句の意味で ── イメージを直接的に表現しない句や、季語がない句である。こうした作品においては、厳格な俳句形式の枠組みの中で捉えるのではなく、作品が持つ真価を味わっていただきたいと考えている。我々が今日理解するところでは、「俳句」という概念と用語は、両方とも19世紀後半まで日本の伝統には存在せず、正岡子規が独立した5-7-5の形式に言及した際、初めてその言葉を使った。それまで5-7-5の形式は、「発句」または「俳諧」と呼ばれ、「連歌(俳諧の連歌)」あるいは「俳文」のような散文物語の長い文学形式に統合されていた。本書は連歌と連歌形式の詩、また俳文を収録している。「モンスーン連歌」は、マレーシアを舞台にした両吟である。

　本書の最終部は、2011年の3月、地震と津波に襲われた東北地方太平洋沿岸を訪れた筆者の見聞をもとに記した俳文である。ここでは、「津波」の内容を明確な季語に代わるものとして考えている。ここで英語の俳句に関わる美学的原則や様々な議論について論じることは控え、日本語でも俳句は決して一次元的ではなく、俳句の巨匠たちでさえも時には規範から逸脱している、というだけに留めておく。芭蕉を例に挙げると、彼も5-5-7や5-9-7の俳句を詠んでいる。作品自体がそれを示し、作品の形式と内容には有機的な結びつきが存在することを望んでやまない。

Note on Translations

The translation of any literary text is no easy matter but translating haiku is especially challenging. The three men cited above—Professor Norifumi Ida, Mr. Hidenori Hiruta and Mr. Ishii Kyoji—all contributed Japanese versions for most or all of the haiku in this collection. Ms. Makiko Hori also made many valuable suggestions. I then sat for many hours with Professor Norifumi Ida to discuss the options and make decisions line by line. We had to balance faithfulness to the original, some approximation of haiku form, and poetic feeling. There are numerous rules and conventions in Japanese haiku that led to prohibitions against certain words or modes of expression. Furthermore, all of these poems, as the book subtitle suggests, are not even intended as haiku but as short poems with some degree of haiku affinity. Haiku is Japan's unique legacy to the literary world, but now it belongs to world literature and will evolve in whatever directions poetic spirit and imagination take it. I hope that in the end the Japanese translations read as poetic compositions, and reflect the beauty of nature and the humanity of human nature.

翻訳について

いかなる文学作品の翻訳も決して易しいものではないが、俳句の翻訳は特に難しい。Norifumi Ida教授、蛭田秀法氏、石井郷二氏の三氏には、この本のすべてないしほとんどの俳句の日本語訳に御尽力をいただいた。また、堀真紀子氏にも多くの貴重な助言を頂いた。さらにNorifumi Ida教授はさらに多くの時間をかけ、私と内容を検討し、一行一行訳を決定してくださった。その中で、英語の原文への忠実さ、俳句の類型性、詩的な印象のについてバランスを整えた。俳句には数多くの規則と慣習があり、特定の言葉や表現が禁じられている。そして、副題が示す通り、この本の全ての詩が、俳句として意図されたわけではなく、俳句にある程度類似した短い詩という意味も込めた。俳句は文学界では他に類を見ない日本固有の遺産であるが、現在では世界文学に属し、詩的な精神と想像力が赴く方向に展開してゆくであろう。本書の日本語訳が最終的には詩的な文章として読まれ、人間性や人間の本質を表すものとなれば幸いである。

Acknowledgments

I would like to acknowledge the work of the translators, Professor Norifumi Ida, Mr. Hidenori Hiruta and Mr. Ishii Kyoji for their time, effort and skills they devoted to this book. I will make a separate comment on the translation process, but the work of these men is greatly appreciated. Also of great assistance in reading and evaluating the translations was Makiko Hori, my former student, whose work is truly appreciated. Next I want to thank Jeannette Brown and Paul Smedberg, who did the design work for the book and who showed great sensitivity to the nature of the material and to the need to present the poems and prose works in as visually pleasing a manner as possible. I also thank my friend Gary Pool, and Banta & Pool Literary Properties, for their support in getting the book into print, and for the support they have given to my work over the years. I would also like to note that several of these haiku previously appeared, usually in slightly different forms, in *Geography of the Soul*, Mellon Poetry Press, 1999 and *Simplicity*, Banta and Pool Literary Properties, 2002—both books written by Kirby Record. Finally, I want to express my thanks for Professor Hiroyuki Kozawa's careful reading of the English text and the Japanese translations, and his many invaluable suggestions.

よもすがら

All Night Long

A Welcome Coolness
from Akita Prefecture

秋田より爽涼を迎えて

a sudden breeze
in bright winter sunlight, leaves
a welcome coolness

冬日差す
そよ風嬉し
心地よさ

in the rain
cherry blossoms start
falling faster

雨降りに
誘われ散りゆく
さくらかな

an empty house
only pictures on the wall
spring rain

空の家
壁に残る絵
春の雨

turning
the curve of her waist
in spring light

春光に　腰の曲線　回りけり

spring rain
futon on tatami
mozart faintly

春の雨
蒲団敷かれて
モーツァルト

april rains
many shades of all-white stones
rushing water

四月の雨　真白き石に　水流る

after the storm
ferns in the windowsill
turn gold

嵐過ぎ
黄金になりし
窓台の羊歯

back from a walk
the sharp scent of weed
on tattered blue jeans

散歩より帰り
強き草の香
ぼろジーンズ

first hike of spring
following another's shadow
resting on my own

春ハイク
人影辿りて
我が影に

summer breeze
ripples mountains in the water
of the rice paddy

夏のそよ風
稲田の水面
さざ波の立つ

indian summer
the monarch and marigold
in fields of weeds

小春日に
マリーゴールドと大樺斑
草の野に

sleeper car
the racketty clacking of rails
october rain

寝台車
レールの響き
十月の雨

first october frost
just cold enough to feel good
with hands in pockets

十月の初霜
ポケットに手の温もり
心地よし

japanese maple
brighter than bright sunlight
all around it

紅葉葉の
日の光を
浴びてさらに眩し

autumn moon glowing
nearly as bright as the sun
sinks into sunset

秋の月　落日のごと　輝きて

the autumn colors
on those nearby mountains, blur
into pure whiteness

山もみじ
霞かかりて
真白にぞ

climbing the mountain
how quickly it is passing
forty-sixth autumn

山路にて　過ごせし秋も　四十六

late october rain,
ice on the rice field's stubble:
orange persimmons

十月末の雨
稲の刈り株氷り張り
オレンジ色の柿

hospital visit –
bright, white walls only deepen
winter's sadness

病院見舞う
明るき白壁
冬の悲しみ深くなり

the grays of twilight:
just above a snow-capped hedge,
orange umbrella

灰色の黄昏　雪被りし垣根の上の　オレンジ色の傘

on the window pane
the rain remains frozen
in the wind's direction

窓ガラス
風に合わせて
雨氷りおり

at the sea's edge
i stare into nothing
tasting snowflakes

渚にて　何も見えずに　雪の味

japanese maple:
falling snow only darkens
its crimson branches

イロハもみじ
降る雪に暗みゆく
深紅の枝葉

in this empty room
i draw back curtains to let in
cold winter stars

空き部屋に
招き入れんとカーテン開く
寒き冬の星々

snow begins to fall
on fields already whitened
by a flock of swans

白鳥の
群れて真白なる畑に
雪が降り

a woman's shadow
across an icy rice field
keeps calling a cat

女の影　氷りし稲田を越えて　猫を呼ぶ

icy rain
on thawing snow
tiny holes

氷雨降る　解けゆく雪の　小穴かな

winter dawn
old man on bicycle pulls
dogs on a leash

冬早朝(ふゆあした) 自転車の老人　犬を曳く

first buds of winter:
beads of ice glow faintly red
japanese maple

冬の初蕾　仄かに赤い氷の珠に　イロハもみじ

frigid monochromes
snow, sky plunging, waves breaking
splinter white ice

極寒の単色画
雪雲垂れて波砕け
砕けゆく白き氷

the december sea
through the clouds barely an opening
for a tiny sunset

師走の海
小さき雲間に
のぞく夕焼け

breaths
white and shapeless
rice fields deep in snow

息白し
雪の深田の
姿なく

sun bursts forth
my shadow blackens
on fresh snow

日がのぞき
わが影黒く
白き新雪

ice on stone
each breath pain
blowing back again

石氷る
息つくたびに
戻る痛さに

snowflakes tumbling down
　　　　but never reaching water
the outdoor onsen

粉雪や
湯には届かず
露天風呂

so scarlet a leaf—
wondering from where it came
to fields deep in snow

深紅の一葉　何処から来たのか　雪深い野に

The Train I'm On:
A Journey Through Japan

車窓から　日本縦断の旅

autumn night and rain
from my window I can see
just the train I'm on

秋の夜の雨
窓から見えるは
我が列車のみ

lilac and pine
beyond the sign marked
"do not enter"

ライラックと松
「入るべからず」の
標識在り

swaying together
the photographer's shadow
and pink water lilies

ともに揺れる
写真家の影と
ピンクのスイレン

willows are bending
round the bend of the river
toward the waterfall

柳が曲がりおり　川の角　滝に向かいて

even after rain
the slight breeze just blows the heat
from there to here

雨止んで
微かな風の
熱誘う

as summer lingers
the waterfall plunges faster:
mogami river

夏残り
滝落ち速し
最上川

misty august rain
as fishermen stand and stare:
water over rock

霧の葉月　岩の上の漁師　見つめる水面

under a street lamp
the gold glow of a firefly
suddenly goes out

街灯に
金色の螢のひかり
こつ然と消えし

streaks of silver lap
the island's flush of green
tiny spirit house

白き小波の縞模様緑なす小島に小さき祠

a shrine to Basho –
where he wrote of silence pierced –
crowded with tourists

芭蕉翁訪ひし跡　染み入る静けさに　人の群れ

two shadows crossing,
as scarlet dragonflies light
on a bamboo pole

二つの影の交わりて
赤とんぼのとまる
竹の竿

water, rock and pine
in the swelter of august
gold of kinkakuji

水、岩、松
茹だる暑さの八月に
金閣寺の金色

blushing rose-purple,
a strutting, hopping pigeon
pursues a mate

赤紫に
一羽の鳩が気取り跳ねて
連れを追う

from a lakeside stall
buying sticky rice on sticks
in the august heat

湖畔の露店(みせ)より
五平餅を買う
八月の暑さに

hopping to my door
a tiny frog pauses, and when
it opens, enters

ピョンピョンと
小さきカエル立ち止まり
開けし戸口に入りくる

in his dream of her
across the august rice fields
silver butterflies

彼の夢の中
彼女は葉月の稲田飛ぶ
銀の蝶

at the very top
of a foggy river bank:
single cicada

霧深く
土手の高みに
一匹の蝉

at ryoanji
stones in sand and all in shadow
the autumn twilight

竜安寺
砂に石すべては影の
秋の黄昏

sliver of moon on
the river's silver ripples
september sunset

白き月　川面の白きさざ波に　長月の入り日

on the sign "Junk Street"
perching at six AM sharp
these glaring crows

「ジャンクストリート」の標識に
朝も六時に止まりおる
睨みをきかすカラスども

cold autumn rain
flowing over blacktop streets,
into a rainbow

冷たい雨の秋
黒きアスファルトの通りを流れ
虹に入る

fading cries of geese
and the scent of mountain pine:
raindrop through the mist

掠れ行く雁の声　山の松の匂い　霧をとおして雨の落つ

our bullet train
pierces the tunnel's darkness
into blinding snow

新幹線　トンネルの暗闇抜けて　雪の眩しさへ

lightning and thunder
rattle the trees, and scatter
snow on top of snow

稲妻と雷
木々を揺さぶり
雪の上にさらにまた雪

the moonlit mountain –
a train whistle fades into
the sound of snow

山を照らす月明かり　汽笛消えゆく　雪のこだまに

how like a dog
he comes running to my door
my neighbors' cat!

犬さながらに
ドアに駆けくる
隣の猫

japanese garden
stones-in-sand and piercing cold
together with us

日本の石庭
砂の石と染み入る寒さ
我らと共に

a sudden shadow
on the snow from the pine grove
becoming crow

にわかに影さして　松林から雪の上　カラスが一羽

hundreds of crows
form a thick long shadow
on the fresh bright snow

群れカラス
黒く影満つ
雪の眩しさ

under snow caps
a blue mountain is swaying
with the drifting mist

雪冠り　揺れる青山　漂う靄

both rain and snow
falling at the same time
on the same place

雨と雪　同時に降って　同じ場所

bullet train quickens
echoing through the tunnel
snowflakes at twilight

新幹線
トンネルの響き
薄暮の雪

black is black
tree at night above the snow
white is white

黒は黒
雪の上に夜の木々
白は白

blurring past,
only a rabbit's footprints
traced in the snow

朧なり
うさぎの足跡
雪の上

filling with snowflakes
beside an empty dog house
a weathered rice bowl

雪一面
空の犬小屋
色あせし碗

something keeps falling
brushing against the *shoji*
shadows of snowflakes

降りたるは
障子を掠って
雪の影

above the sea
sunset about to snow
a brilliant white

海の上
夕日に降り出す
白銀の雪

a ray of sunset
leaves a trace of crimson
on ordinary snow

夕映えの
深紅の色あり
いつもの雪に

winter solitude
in white tips of pine needles
i can see the wind

冬寂し
白き松葉に
風のあと

東京の露しずく

Tokyo
Dewdrops

nocturnal neon
    lights up a silver dewdrop
        tokyo spring

夜のネオン
    銀の露照らす
        東京の春

        the pond in spring
        bubbles from a boy's pipe
        the colors of carp

        春の池
        こどものシャボンに
        鯉の色

    stirring spring colors
        from the bottom of the pond
    carp totally white

春色を　池底からそよがす　白き鯉

        bowing together
        leaning away from the storm
        pink hollyhocks

        一斉に頭を垂れて
        嵐から
        ピンクのタチアオイ

beads of summer rain
      cling to a metal railing
           and fall one by one

夏雨のしずく
      手すりに纏わり
           ポタリポタリと

      carp pond
fish eyes always staring
      peonies

         池の鯉
      見つめる先に
芍薬の花

reaching for a hat
      between points of stillness
           summer wind quickens

急な夏風に
      帽子取られて
           手を伸ばす

university night class
the sweet-potato vender
chanting his mantra

大学の夜授業
石焼き芋の
唱えるマントラ

blinking airplane lights
suddenly disappear
under the full moon

満月に
突然かすむ
飛行機の灯

sweeping leaves
just ahead of the street cleaner
september wind

葉っぱ掃く
街路掃除の前を
九月の風

in the icy wind
rushing raincoats blurred
by swirling snowflakes

凍る風　渦巻く雪に　コートがぼやけ

a biting wind
　　　the shop's thin shoji
　　　　　still serving cold soba

凍てつく風
　　　障子張りの店に
　　　　　今も出る冷やし蕎麦

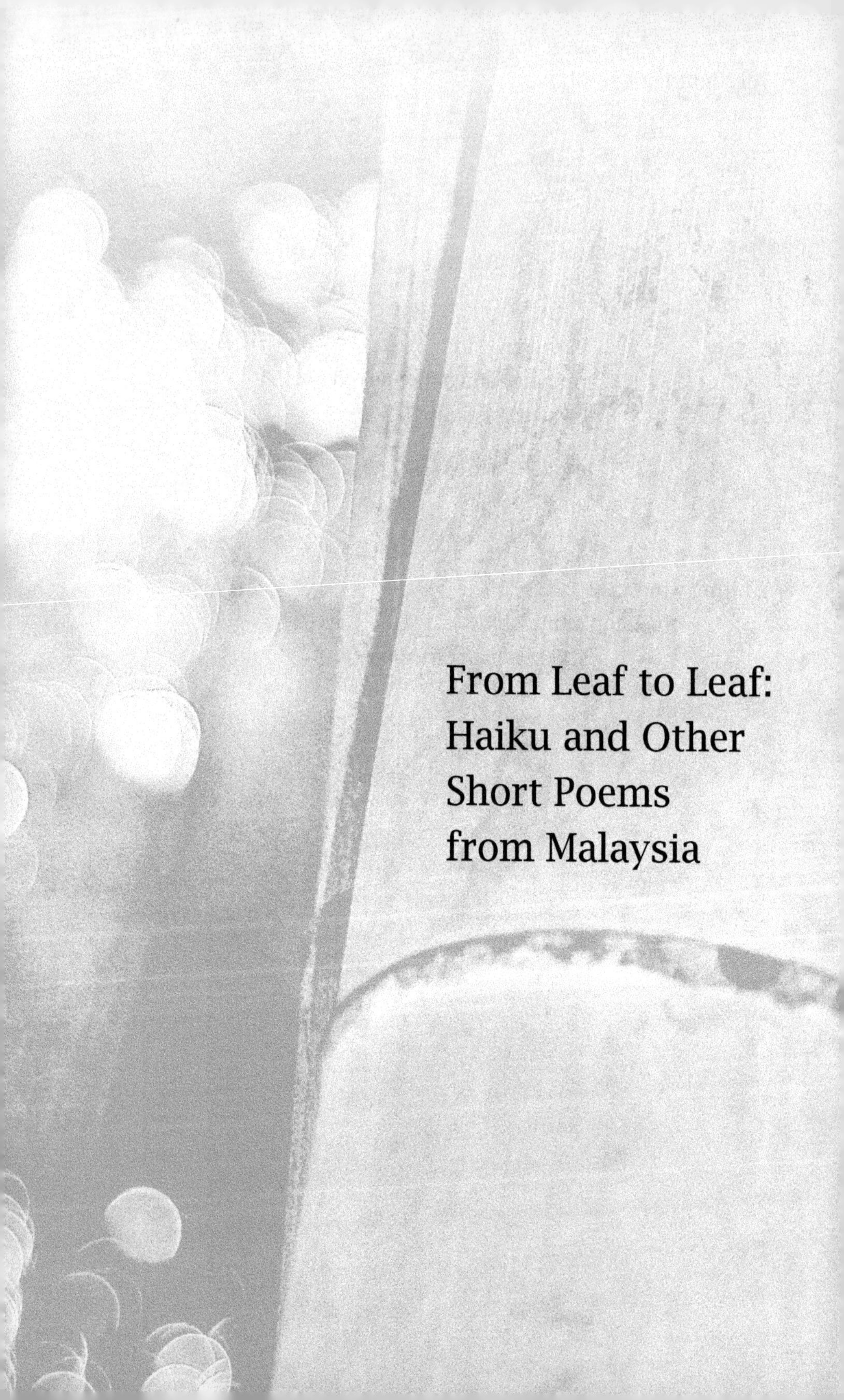

From Leaf to Leaf: Haiku and Other Short Poems from Malaysia

葉から葉へ　俳句と短詩

マレーシア編

all night long
a single drop of rain
from leaf to leaf

よもすがら
雨のしずくが
葉から葉へ

coconut crashes
from its dark silhouette
into moonlight

ココナッツ　闇より落ちて　月明かり

bamboos leaning
in the wind's direction
slimmer in the rain

雨の中
風吹く向きに
靡く竹

summer afternoon:
evening begins edging
out of the forest

夏の午後　森から縁どる　夕べかな

under yellow skies
very yellow parasols,
and rustling dresses

黄の空に　真っ黄色な傘　ドレスの擦れる音

face cool and pale:
moonlight trailing after her
blackened silhouette

顔白く
月のひかり彼女追う
影黒く

slow rain patters
on the patio orchids
of green branches

雨したたる　中庭の蘭の　青い枝

severed orchid stems –
she vows revenge on every
snail of the night

茎切られし
蘭の恨みは
夜の蝸牛

waking to a storm
that shatters a closed window
in my dream of you

窓打つ嵐にきみの夢破れ

waking
to sticky cobwebs
on my face

目が覚めて
蜘蛛の巣絡む
我が顔に

after the rain stops
lightning-flashes still light up
raindrops here and there

雨上がり
なお続く稲妻に
ここもかしこも光る雨だれ

a bird plunges
the blue of the sky
on its wings

鳥一羽　空の青さに　翼飛ぶ

the crimson orchids
i've taken you here to see
dried up since morning

深紅の蘭
見せたくも
朝より乾きはて

dewy window pane
all the milky day a boy
sits watching the rain

霧の窓　少年が白き一日　雨を見る

each fresh drop of rain
ripples a banana frond
to its very stalk

降る雨に
茎まで揺れる
バナナの葉

orchid, stem and leaf
upright in a pot beneath
the Milky Way

蘭の茎葉　鉢の下には　天の川

how different each sounds -
from one drop to another -
raindrops on the roof

一滴毎の
異なる音に
屋根の雨

a month of rain
i hear only the pauses
between the drops

雨の月
耳に残るは
滴の合間の小休止

mother in law
fallen asleep where she sits
still munching peanuts

義理の母
座りたままに眠り入り
なおポリポリと落花生

clutching umbrellas
grandmothers pursue small boys
through the monsoon rain

傘握り
孫追う祖母たち
モンスーン

falling on
flowering asters
falling star

落ちてくる
花咲くアスターに
流れ星

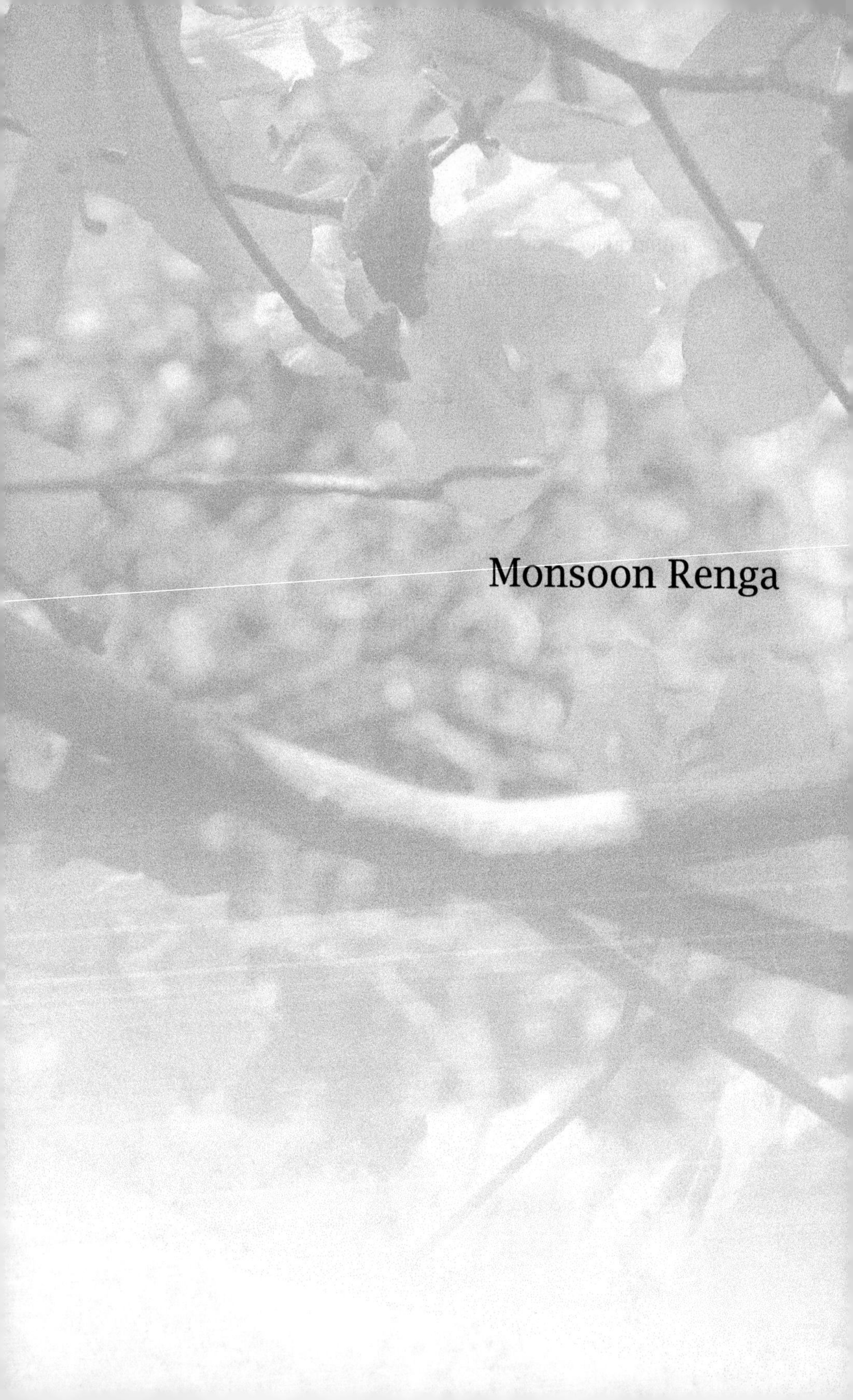

Monsoon Renga

連歌　モンスーン　（両吟）

after rain, soft glow
of white skies; gold sun, falling
on red earth like rain

                in another place and time
                autumn leaves turning to snow

turning as dreams turn
timeless and sudden, the rains
deluge the mind's heart

                shattering blue afternoons
                like love's beginning or end

look upon gardens
tailored swirl of stem in bloom
look upon rivers

                on burial by quicksand
                there resides the monsoon's blood

driving through monsoon
traffic bumper to bumper
far as eyes can see

                mist smoking off jungle tops
                sunset's orange ball burns bright

first one drop falling—
then in twos and threes and fours
the monsoon gathers

                such brief warning in its birth
                so sudden its cessation

雨の後、白い空
柔らかな輝き；金色の光、降りくる
雨のように赤土に

　　　　　別な場所別な時には
　　　　　秋の葉が変わり雪になる

夢の如く巡り
時ならず突然に
雨が溢れる心

　　　　　心乱れる鬱な午後
　　　　　恋の始まりや終わりの如く

庭を見て
渦仕立ての花の茎
川を見て

　　　　　流砂に埋もれて
　　　　　モンスーンのいのち

モンスーンの中を
バンパー擦り寄せ
目の届く所　車が走る

　　　　　密林の煙る霞に
　　　　　夕日にオレンジ色のボールが
　　　　　燃え

最初の一滴
続いて二つ三つ四つ
モンスーン来る

　　　　　いとも短き発生の警告
　　　　　その停止　いとも突然

bombs of the monsoon
drop on empty parking lots
drench crows on tree limbs

                    suddenly the sky stands still
                    above hospital-white walls

the wards are silent
and dingy, scrubbed thinly grey
rain drops fall singly

                    beds of the dead and dying
                    form rows of white rectangles

i rush for the car
trying to beat the downpour
standing there, you shrug

                    "it's only monsoon again
                    but father must be dying"

rain darkens pavement
flocks of crows rise up flapping
their cries, black on grey

                    head-first into the cloudburst
                    so quickly their wingtips fade

in autumn deluge
i thought i saw peonies
scattering plumage

                    on the grey sky's other side
                    seeing dreams of silk azure

モンスーンの爆弾
空の駐車場に落ちて
大枝の鳥を濡らす

        突然空が静まり
        病院の白壁の上に

静まる病棟
暗く洗い流せし薄灰色の
雨の滴ポツリと

        亡くなりし人と死に向かう人たちの
        ベッドの白き長方形の列

急ぎ車に向かい
土砂降りを逃れる私に
きみは立ちしまま肩を竦める

        「またモンスーンが来ただけさ
        だが父は死にかかっている」

雨に道暗くなり
鳥の群飛び上がり
灰色に黒く　叫び声

        雲間に頭から
        忽ち翼端が消え

秋の豪雨に
羽毛を撒き散らす
芍薬を見たと思ひしが

        灰色の空の向こうに
        紺碧の絹の夢見て

Scattered Hyacinth:
Haiku, and
Other Short Poems
from America

撒き散らされしヒヤシンス

俳句と短詩 アメリカ編

after the storm
blackbirds fly down to strut
on scattered hyacinth

嵐去り
散らばるヒヤシンスに
椋鳥誇らしげ

magnolia blossoms
piling up in the garden
thoughts of my mother

モクレンの花
庭に積み重なりて
母思う

earthy scent of rain
by blooming rhododendron,
a basketball hoop

土匂う雨　花咲くシャクナゲ　バスケの輪

roses are blooming
from the shadow of the cat
in the flower pot

植木鉢猫の影から薔薇が咲く

stretching a front paw
from fence down to flower pot
home again comes cat

前爪を伸ばし
フェンスから植木鉢に飛び下り
猫また家に戻る

black and white photo
sweet taste of honeysuckle
childhood summer

白黒の写真
スイカズラの甘い風味
子どもの頃の夏

in the twilight glow
spider on its silver thread
descends on a rose

黄昏に
銀糸辿って
薔薇に蜘蛛

we look and are gone
in the spot where we once stood
an iris and a stone

ちらっと見て
かつてのここに
アイリスと石

around the spot where
the august moon is hiding
the clouds glow whiter

その辺り
8月の月隠れ
雲白く輝く

new york nocturne
yellow cabs rushing past
flowers in the rain

ニューヨーク夜想曲
黄色いタクシーが急ぎ行く
雨中の花

messages to lost ones
photos tied to a rusting fence
september eleven

亡き者へのメッセージ
錆びたフェンスに写真の数々
9月の11日

covering every inch
on the path to the station
beige-on-scarlet leaves

一面に覆いし駅道に赤茶色の葉

pianist
the lips constantly moving—
to a wordless tune

ピアニスト
歌詞のない曲に
唇の絶えざる動き

a winter night's dream
my thoughts wander aimlessly:
neither here nor there

冬の夜の夢に彷徨う我が思い

in the subway car
tapping ice off his white cane
old man begs for alms

地下鉄で　白杖叩き氷落とし　老人恵み乞う

after a cold hard rain
under December sunlight:
luminous sidewalks

寒く激しい雨が止み
師走の陽の下
歩道が光る

"World Trade Center"
faded sign in the subway:
loneliness

世界貿易センター
地下鉄の標識薄れ
うら寂し

in the chill of night
shadow on the kitchen wall
the shape of a rat

夜の寒きに　キッチンの壁に　ネズミの形

隻手の声

One Hand Clapping

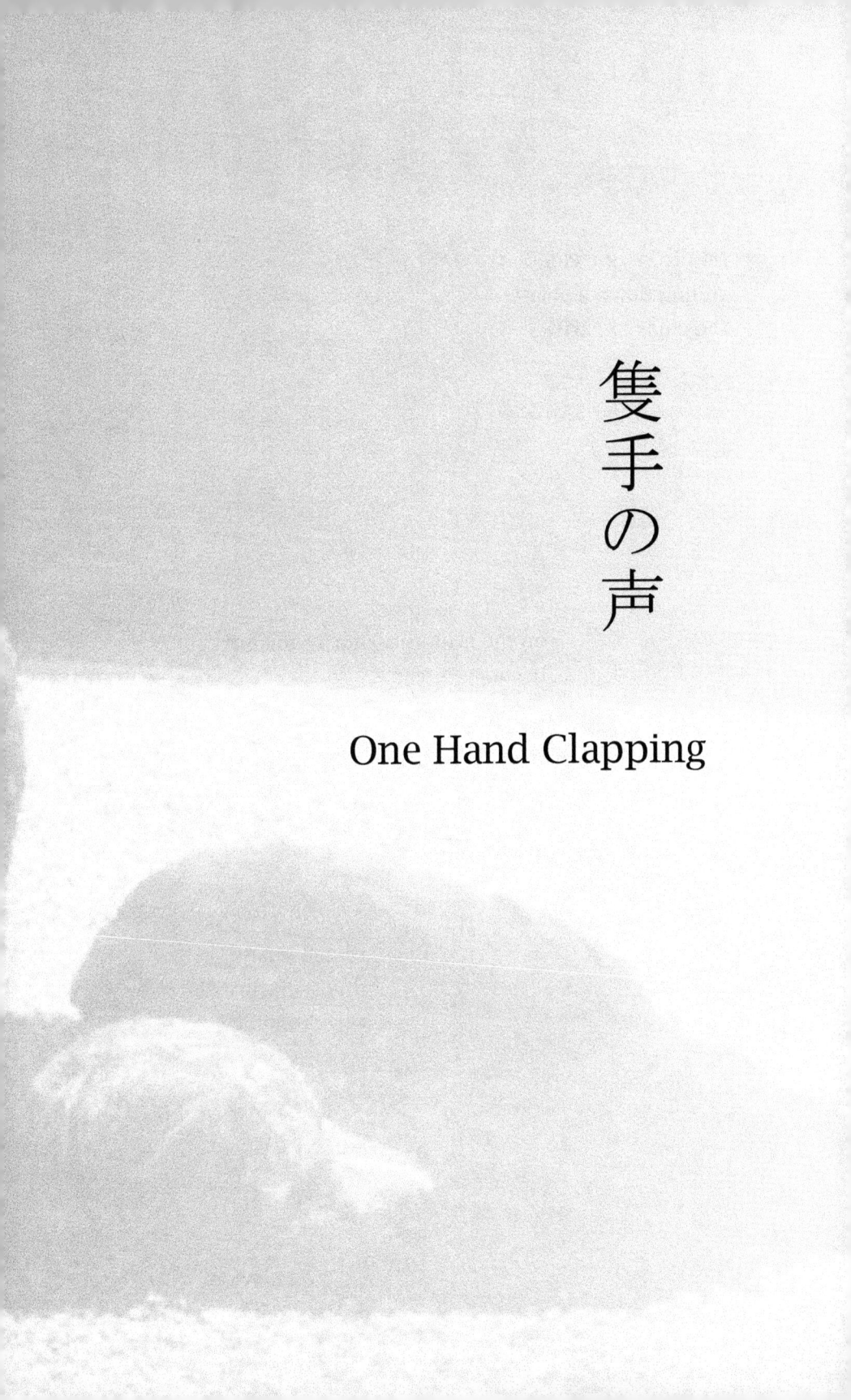

rain from one cloud
sliding down a palette
the color of earth

一つの雲から雨が
パレットを滑り降りる
地の色

a knot in wood
on the sculpture of a young girl
becomes a tear

木の節は
彫刻の少女の
涙になる

whose reality?
this sculpture of a baby
without a face

誰のこと？
幼子のこの彫刻
顔がなく

a boy suckling
looks away from the nipple
with a sudden laugh

乳吸う坊や
乳首から目をそらし
にわかに笑う

two years old –
dressed only in his coat –
wants to go out

2才の子　上着だけ着て　出掛るという

infant son
changed three times since morning
the color of his eyes

幼き息子
朝より3度
目の色を変え

my eyes open –
so dark the cicada's call
in this empty room

目が開く　暗闇に蝉の声　なにもなき部屋

inside their kennels
nine large dogs are staring
at canine sunset

犬小屋で
9匹の大きな犬がじっと見る
犬の夕焼け

dot by dot
the darkness i am staring into
fills up with stars

ひとつひとつ　じっと見つめる闇　星一杯に

old woman
hobbles, pushing a stroller
full of groceries

老女押す
食べもの一杯ベビーカー
心もとなく

whirling snowflakes
suddenly float slow-motion
near the pine forest

渦巻く雪片　突如ゆるりと漂う　松林の近く

email from a friend—
deceased more than half a year—
but can't delete

友のメール
亡くなりて半年余り
削除せず

a boy
on his bridge of dreams
becomes a man

少年
夢の橋の上で
大人になる

at Kisakata
Basho called their home "hell"
 (there's no place like hell)

象潟で
芭蕉は彼らの家を「地獄」と呼んだ
（地獄のようにすてきな所はない）

picture window
turns the whole room gray
a chilling dusk

大窓の
部屋一面を灰色にして
冷える黄昏

with a black leash
a dog is dragging its master
across a snowy field

黒ひもで　主人を引きずる犬あり　雪の原

old woman walking
       bent
       right-
       angle
to earth

老女が
地に腰を直角にし
歩いてる

looking back, i see
her face half shadow, half white:
dazzling moon on snow

振り返りながら、見る
彼女の顔の半分が影、半分が白色：
雪上の眩いまでの月

drop by drop
icicles from my roof
syncopation

一つまた一つ
屋根の氷柱から水が滴る
シンコペーション

november moonlight
sounds i never heard before
hospital room

霜月の月光
初めて聞く音
病の部屋

painful though it is
life gets better and better
colors of autumn

苦しくも
良くなるこの世の
秋の色

a refreshing breeze
as the train accelerates
autumn is passing

そよ風に
電車は加速
秋過ぐる

winter night
the clock from this dream
keeps ticking

冬の夜　この夢の置き時計　カチカチと

my useless zazen
and still i'm hooked on haiku
autumn leaves come down

むなしき座禅　俳句に没頭　木の葉落ち

In Memoriam:
Poems following the Great Earthquake
and Tsunami from the
Tohoku Region of Eastern Honshu

追悼
東日本大震災の爪痕を訪ね俳句を記す

Greener and deeper
The mountain pathways narrow:
Summer is ending

緑濃く
細き山路に
夏過ぎる

Looking down upon
Quietly slogging sea waves
Nothing but rubble

見下ろせば
静かに打ち寄す海の波
瓦礫の他は何もなく

Torn to pieces
On a concrete slab near the sea
A girl's pink slippers

ボロボロに裂けて
海辺のコンクリに
ピンクのスリッパ

Mountains of debris—
What's left of shattered houses
And children's dreams

瓦礫の山　潰れし家と子供らの　夢に何が残りし

A fifty-foot cliff
When the tsunami struck
Nowhere to go

15メートルの崖
津波が来ても
逃げ場なし

A single flower
Household things and splintered wood
All that remains

花一輪
家財に木片
残りしすべて

An empty field
Where a house was standing
A woman praying

すべて失せし原
家のありしところ
祈る女あり

Jutting into the street
A massive ship tossed on shore
The sound of water

通りに突き出たまま
陸に打ち上げられし大型船
波の音

Amid the rubble
A child's helmet, blue and gold
Where are you now?

瓦礫の中に
青と金色、子供用ヘルメット
今きみはどこ？

Row after row
Mangled car chassis gleaming
At the sea's edge

どこまでも並びて
潰れしシャシー光る
海の端

Soft breeze from the sea
The breathing of the living
Silence of the dead

海のそよ風　生ける者の息　死者の沈黙

In the debris
Of a smashed Toyota
"Doraemon"

瓦礫の山
潰れしトヨタ車の中に
「ドラエモン」

Changing shades of green
From mountain after mountain
And then another

山から山へ
移ろう緑陰の
さらなる山へ

Villages of rubble
Everything washed away
But the still-blue sky

瓦礫の村落
何もかも流されて
なお静かなる青い空

Clutched in the hand
Of a child, floating face down—
Her favorite doll

伏せて浮く　子どもの手に大好きな　お人形

Under blue, blue sky
Villages washed out to sea—
Which keeps on rocking

青空の下
海に押し流されし村
揺れ続く

A smashed-car graveyard:
Glowing bright between the cars
Spider webs catch sun

潰れし車の墓場　間の蜘蛛の巣　日を捕え

The white stone goddess
Looks down on the tsunami
Still silent, still still

白石の観音
見下ろす津波になおも語らず
なおも動かず

In Memoriam:
Haibun following the Great Earthquake
and Tsunami from the Tohoku Region
of Eastern Honshu

追悼

東日本大震災の爪痕を訪ね俳文を記す

When the earthquake and tsunami that devastated the eastern Tohoku region of Japan first struck in March of 2011, I happened to be away from my home in Akita, which is on the West coast of Tohoku. Nonetheless, from the tenth floor of a building near Osaka, about 1200 kilometers away from the epicenter, I felt the earth shaking for more than 3 minutes. These are the moments that we remember the rest of our lives, because we could have just as easily been among the more than 25,000 to be lost that day and in the days that followed. The paradox of poetry is to express in words that which cannot be *expressed* at all, but merely pointed to; the additional challenge of haiku is to do this as briefly as possible while still adhering to a set of demanding and precise formal requirements. (This is true even when we are writing so-called "free haiku.") To put the experience of the Great Tohoku Earthquake in words is the task I have set for myself, however hopeless it might seem, because as survivors all we can do is remember and verbal expression of thought and feeling is one of the most precious human-specific traits with which a poet should be especially gifted.

With this in mind, I set out four months later to visit the area of the disaster, and to see for myself what had happened there. No matter how many times we see the horrifying television images of houses, vehicles and people being swept away like so much debris, it conveys only a fraction of the emotional shock that overwhelms the one who ventures to look upon the scene with his or her own eyes.

What struck me first as I approached the Pacific coast, was the stunning beauty of the mountains as they descended to the sea. Then once along the coast line, the bays and coves that curved in and out along beaches were more luminous in light and

indigo in shadow than I had ever seen, a vision to be shattered
moments later when I saw below me scenes of sheer desolation:
hollowed houses and apartment buildings, dream homes
annihilated, cars smashed like giant tin cans, stacked high and
lined up in rows along the beach. It was late July, and the kind of
nostalgia that seems to accompany late summer was visible
through the trees, which in retrospect, seemed to reflect the
certainty that something ineffably precious had been lost forever:

> Greener and deeper
> The mountain pathways narrow:
> Summer is ending

Going from such scenes of impeccable nature to the following
scene happened again and again as I drove south along the
coastal rode toward Sendai.

> Looking down upon
> Quietly slogging sea waves
> Nothing but rubble

Piled up in the rubbish were the tangible pieces of people's
lives, sometimes intact, sometimes in shreds, to be found along
the beach, and in the massive mountains of fragments that have
been bulldozed into desolate fields where once stood the
homes of fishing communities, for many generations having
made their livelihoods from the sea.

> Under blue, blue sky
> Villages washed out to sea
> Which keeps on rocking

And there were also lofty summer dream homes of the more affluent, wiped away or gutted:

> Mountains of debris—
> What's left of shattered houses
> And children's dreams

The poem just cited evokes Basho's masterpiece:

> Summer grasses
> Of those brave warriors' dreams—
> All that's left

Here I might note that in the tradition of Chinese and Japanese poetry undocumented quotations and allusions are common. There is no "anxiety of influence" in these cases, since it was simply assumed that readers were as knowledgeable as writers. Echoing lines from the culture's poetic legacy simply added resonance, and linked today with yesterday in the endless chain of being that flows from every point in time to every other. In this sense, the brevity and imagistic nature of haiku undermines the linear nature of its language in a way longer works cannot: it has words but seems wordless; it flows through time but is timeless. Basho's "Summer Grasses" haiku is evoked once more in this one:

> A single flower
> Household things and splintered wood
> All that remains

The scarred landscape left by the Tohoku earthquake and tsunami has been likened to a battlefield, in which man-made structures and human survival were simply no match for the awesome forces of nature. But in all this heartache and tragedy, contemplation of the fates of the children taken by the devastation is the most intolerable:

> Torn to pieces
> On a concrete slab near the sea
> A girl's pink slippers

Or this:

> Amid the rubble
> A child's helmet, blue and gold
> Where are you now?

It was impossible not to notice how the landscape, once thought as idyllic as paradise, created horrifying deathtraps for the unfortunate victims of the tidal waves:

> A fifty-foot cliff
> When the tsunami struck
> Nowhere to go

The bereaved are still a constant presence, even months later, as expressed so inadequately by this:

> In an empty field
> Where houses and homes once stood
> A woman praying

It is chilling enough to imagine what happened to the people caught in those ravaging walls of water, but for thousands of survivors, there can be no real closure; the bodies of thousands of loved ones have simply disappeared, and will never be found. In some cases, even all public records of their existence are also missing along with photographs and personal effects. Their lives have simply been eradicated except for flames of flickering memories.

One of the most publicized scenes of the disaster was that of an enormous cargo ship tossed 200 meters from the beach through a tall concrete wall and into a street. What one must imagine here is the enormity of the vessel that towers above the shoulder-high wall and the people gathered around it.

> Jutting into the street
> A massive ship tossed on shore
> The sound of water

This poem plays in a bitterly ironical way with the final line of the most famous haiku of all:

> An old pond
> As a frog jumps in
> The sound of water

Whereas with Basho's haiku the "sound of water" leads to the tranquility of an eternal silence, in this case the monotonously soothing sound of the tide recalls the roaring of the sea at its most lethal. Indeed there is no sound more varied than that of water.

Some of the eeriest scenes along the Pacific coast of Tohoku are those of smashed vehicles of all kinds and shapes stacked three or four high in row after row like stones in a graveyard. These are slightly reminiscent of American junkyards with rusted cars in rows and stacks.

> Row after row
> Mangled car chassis gleaming
> At the sea's edge

> A smashed-car graveyard:
> Glowing bright between the cars
> Spider webs catch sun

But there is a horrendous difference here between these cars and those of an ordinary junkyard. These flattened cars remain today as they were just after the waters raged over and under them, with personal items of their owners still inside, including clothing, toys, and other effects. Of these I will mention a small plastic *Doraemon* toy, a comb, a purse, a cell phone, and a tattered address book.

> In the debris
> Of a smashed Toyota
> "Doraemon"

In the end there is nothing to do but hope that the survivors find a way to go on living happy and productive lives, and that Japan recovers someday from this nightmare. One thing this event has shown to the world is the dignity and resilience of the Japanese people. As one person said to me, Japanese have always lived with the knowledge that earthquakes, tsunami and hurricanes are possible almost anywhere on their beautiful islands. They live in constant awareness of the brevity of life, hence their often unconscious affinity to a Buddhist outlook, which embraces the here and now more confidently than it speculates about an afterlife. This may explain why Japanese are more sensuous and down to earth about physical pleasures than people of many other cultures. Life is not somewhere else or some other time, and many believe that there can be no spirit without a physical presence.

> A breeze from the sea
> The breathing of the living
> Silence of the dead

They have their gods and goddesses, their mythologies and superstitions, like everyone else, but more often than not, these deities are beautiful, silent and indifferent:

> The white stone goddess
> Looks down on the tsunami
> Still silent, still still

And yet the sea rocks in its cradle, as benign as it is malignant, as life giving as it is deadly. The mountains also have spirits (and bodies) of their own, beyond the passions, joys and suffering of humankind.

> Changing shades of green
> From mountain after mountain
> And then another

This is how the world has always been and will always be, but to remain human we grieve, we honor; we remember, but live on, as long as time allows us.

2011年3月11日、日本の東北地方を荒廃させた大地震と津波が最初に襲ったとき、私は偶然にも、秋田の自宅から遠く離れたところにいた。震源地から約1,200キロ離れた大阪近郊にあるビルの10階で、3分以上の間、地面が揺れ動くのを感じた。生涯忘れ得ぬ瞬間であった。あの日、そしてその後の日々に命を失った、25,000以上の人々のうちの一人に、いとも簡単になり得たからである。

　　詩のパラドックスは、言葉で表現することは到底できない事象を、単に言葉を並べて表現することにある。さらに難しいのは、厳しく緻密な形式の条件に従いつつ、できる限り簡潔にこれを実行することである。(このことは、私たちがいわゆる「自由俳句」を作っている時でさえも当てはまる)。東日本大震災の経験を言葉で表現することは、途方もないことの様に思える。しかし、生き残った者として私たちができることは、ひとえに記憶することであり、思いや感情を言葉で表すことは、人間だけに与えられた最も尊い能力である。詩を心得たものは、その特性に長けているはずだ、という考えのもと、この務めを自分自身に課した。

　　このことを心に留め、4ヵ月後、私は災害のあった場所を訪れるべく家を出たのであった。そこで何が起こったのかを、自らの目で確かめたかったのである。家や車や人々がゴミくずのごとく押し流されてゆく恐ろしい光景を繰り返しテレビで見ても、それが伝えるものは、自らの目で現場を見る者を圧倒する、精神的衝撃のほんの一部にすぎないのである。

　　太平洋岸に近づいて最初に受けた印象は、海へと傾斜する山々の衝撃的な美しさだった。そして海岸線に出てみると、見え隠れしながら岸辺の曲線を描く湾や入り江は、それまでに見たことがないほどの輝く光と藍色の影にあふれていた。しかしその景色は、一瞬の後に、眼下にみる破壊し尽くされた光景により、粉々になった。ポッカリと空ろな家屋やアパ

ート、壊滅した夢のマイホーム、巨大なブリキ缶のように潰された車などが、海岸に沿って高く積み上げられ列をなしていた。7月の下旬だった。晩夏に起こるような一種の郷愁が、木々を通して垣間見られ、振り返ると、言葉では言い尽くせないほど貴重ななにかが、永遠に失われてしまったという事実を伝えているように思えた。

　　　緑濃く
　　　細き山路に
　　　夏過ぎる

非の打ちどころのない自然のそのような光景から、次のような景色が次々と現れたのは、私が海岸沿いの道を仙台に向かって南へと車で移動しているときだった。

　　　見下ろせば
　　　静かに打ち寄す海の波
　　　瓦礫の他は何もなく

積み上げられた廃物は、人々の生活のかけらである。海岸に沿って、無傷のものもあれば、引き裂かれたものもあり、ブルドーザーで荒涼とした土地に押しやられてできた、巨大な瓦礫の山と化している。そこは、それまで何世代にも亘って海からの恵みで生計を立ててきた、漁師の家々が立ち並んでいた場所である。

　　　青空の下
　　　海に押し流されし村
　　　揺れ続く

そこにはまた、裕福な人々の格調ある別荘も並んでいたが、
津波に一掃され、すっかり破壊されてしまっていた。

> 瓦礫の山
> 潰れし家と子らの夢
> 何が残りし

上に引用した句は、芭蕉の傑作を思い起こさせる。

> 夏草や
> 兵どもが
> 夢の跡

中国と日本の詩の伝統では、引用や引喩の典拠を明示しな
いのが慣例であることに注目したい。この場合「影響の懸念」
は全くない。というのも、読者は書き手と同じくらいに知識が
あるものと思われてきたからである。同じ文化の詩的遺産から
数行まねたとしても、それは単に共鳴を繰り返したに過ぎず、
ある時点から別の時点へと流れる果てしない連鎖の中で、今
日と昨日とを結びつけたのである。この意味で、俳句の簡潔
さと写象主義的な性格が、長編詩にはできない方法で言語
が持つ直鎖的な性質を弱めるのである。言葉で表現するもの
の、言葉が無いように感じる、時間を通して流れるが超越もし
ている。芭蕉の「夏草や」の俳句が、次の句でもう一度呼び起
される。

> 花一輪
> 家財に木片
> 残りしすべて

東北地方大地震と津波の爪痕は、戦場にも例えられてきた。
そこでは、人間が建てた建造物も、人の生存も、自然の恐る
べき力の前では無力でしかない。しかし、この心痛む悲劇に
あって、その惨害に打ちのめされた子供たちの運命を考える
と、耐え難いことこのうえない。

　　　　　粉々に裂けた
　　　　　海辺のコンクリートに
　　　　　小さなピンクのスリッパ

また:

　　　　　瓦礫のなか
　　　　　青と金、子供用のヘルメット
　　　　　いまきみはどこ?

かつては楽園さながらの牧歌的風景が、不運にも津波の犠牲
となった人たちにとって、いかに恐るべき死の淵となったか、
その印象は余りにも強烈過ぎた。

　　　　　15メートルの崖
　　　　　津波が来ても
　　　　　逃げ場なし

残された人々の姿は、数か月経っても消えることがない。言葉
で言い表しても意を尽くせないが—

　　　　　すべて失せし原
　　　　　かつて家のありしところ
　　　　　祈る女あり

すべてを打ち砕く水の壁から逃げられなかった人々に何が起こったかを想像するだけで背筋が寒くなるが、生き残った大勢の人たちにとって、本当の意味での終わりが無いことも恐ろしい。何千もの愛する人たちの体が完全に消えてしまい、これからも見つかることはないだろう。写真や個人の所有物とともに、彼らの存在を証明する公的な記録さえもが、全て無くなってしまったケースもある。彼らの命は、かすかな思い出の光を残してすべて消し去られてしまった。

　　　災害の爪痕の光景でもっとも報道されたものの一つは、海岸から高いコンクリートの塀を越えて200メートル離れた通りにまで打ち上げられた巨大な貨物船である。ここで注目すべきは、人の肩ほどの高さの壁やそれを見に集まった人々の上にそびえる船の巨大さである。

　　　　　通りに突き出たまま
　　　　　陸に打ち上げられし大型船
　　　　　波の音

この句は、歴代のなかで最も著名な俳句の結句を極めて皮肉を込めて捩っている。

　　　　　古池や
　　　　　蛙飛びこむ
　　　　　水の音

芭蕉の句では、「水の音」が、いつまでも静かであるという落ち着きに通じるのに対して、ここでは、波の単調で和ませる音が最も破壊的になったときの海のとどろきを呼び起す。確かに、水の音ほど変化に富んでいる音はない。

　　　東北地方の太平洋岸に沿って目に入る最も悍ましい
光景のなかには、まるで霊園の墓石のように三層四層に積み
重なった様々な種類や形の潰れた車の姿がある。それは、錆
びた車が何列にも積み重なっているアメリカの廃品置場にも
少々似ている。

　　　　　　なん列も
　　　　　　ねじれし車台光る
　　　　　　海の端

　　　　　　潰れし車の墓場
　　　　　　間の蜘蛛の巣
　　　　　　日を捕え

だが、こうした車と普段見掛ける廃車処理場の車とには、恐ろ
しいほどの違いがある。この押しつぶされた車は、波が押し寄
せ、その上下でうねった時のまま残っているし、車内には衣類
や玩具、身の回りのものなど、オーナーの所有物が残ってい
る。その中でも、小さなプラスティックのドラエモン人形、櫛、
財布、携帯電話そして、ぼろぼろになった住所録が印象に残
る。

　　　　　　潰れしトヨタ車
　　　　　　残骸の中に
　　　　　　「ドラエモン」

結局、生き残った人たちがなんとか幸せで豊かな生活を見出
し、いつの日か日本がこの悪夢から立ち直ることを願うほかなす
術が無い。この出来事が世界に示したことのひとつは、日
本国民の気品と回復力である。ある人が私に言ったが、日本

人は、いつも地震、津波そして台風が、この美しい島々のど
こでも起こりうるというということを意識しながら生きてきた。彼
らは、常に、人生の儚さを意識して生きているため、死後の世
界について考えを巡らすより、自信を持って、ここ、この時、と
いった現実を受け入れるという仏教の考え方に意識しなくて
も親近感を持つのである。このことは、何故、日本人がほかの
文化に生きる多くの人々よりも、身体的な喜びについて感覚
的に鋭敏で現実的である、という説明になるのかもしれない。
人生は、どこか他の所や他の時間にあるのではない。多くの
人たちは、肉体が存在しなければ魂も存在し得ない、と信じ
ている。

　　　　海のそよ風
　　　　生ける者の息
　　　　死者の沈黙

彼らには他と同じように、神や女神があり、神話や迷信がある
が、ほとんどの場合、神々は美しく、語らず、公平である。

　　　　白石の観音
　　　　見下ろす津波になおも語らず
　　　　なおも動かず

それでもなお、海は、その地でうねり、悪意に満ちていると思
えば慈悲深く、命を奪うと思えば与えもする。山々にも、人間
の情熱や喜び、そして苦悩を越えて魂（と姿）がある。

　　　　山から山へ
　　　　移ろう緑陰の
　　　　さらなる山へ

この世は、これまでかくあり、これからもかくあるだろう。しかし、人であり続けるために、我々は、嘆き悲しみ、讃え、記憶し、時間が許す限り生き続ける。

Biography

Kirby Record was born in 1947 in the state of Indiana, USA. He studied classics, linguistics and literature at Indiana University where he earned three degrees. He has lectured at numerous universities in America, Malaysia and Japan, including Indiana University, Harvard University, Showa Women's University, Keio University and Akita International University. He is a poet, has published three previous books of poems, many essays, and eight books on language, language-teaching materials and literature. Previous books of poetry include *A Geography of the Soul*, Edwin Poetry Press, 1999, and *Simplicity, Poetry and Photography*, Banta and Pool, 2002. In November of 2014, his postmodern fiction, *The Mysterious Frog in the Mountains of the Six Excellencies*—co-authored with Lucas Christopoulos—will be published by Moon Willow Press. He took the photographs used throughout this book. He is currently working as the Director of Language Programs and as a professor at Yamanashi Gakuin University.

* 9 7 8 0 9 6 6 7 2 3 7 3 1 *